Wreckage

Other Books by Ha Jin

Poetry

Between Silences, University of Chicago, 1990
Facing Shadows, Hanging Loose, 1996

Prose

Ocean of Words, Zoland, 1996
    (winner, PEN/Hemingway Award)
Under the Red Flag, University of Georgia, 1997
    (winner, Flannery O'Connor Award)
In the Pond, Zoland, 1998
Waiting, Pantheon, 1999 (winner, National Book Award
    and PEN/Faulkner Award)
The Bridegroom, Pantheon, 2000

Wreckage

HA JIN

Hanging Loose Press
Brooklyn, New York

Published by Hanging Loose Press, 231 Wyckoff Street, Brooklyn, New York 11217. All Rights Reserved. No part of this book may be reproduced without the publisher's written permission, except for brief quotations in reviews.

Hanging Loose Press thanks the Literature Program of the New York State Council on the Arts and the Fund for Poetry for grants in support of this book's publication.

Printed in the United States of America
10 9 8 7 6 5 4 3 2 1

Some of these poems first appeared in the following magazines: *Agni, The American Voice, Atlanta Review, Bombay Gin, Boulevard, Crab Orchard Review, Crazyhorse, Gulf Stream, Hanging Loose, International Poetry Quarterly, The Kenyon Review, Manoa, New England Review, New Letters, Patagonian Winds, Prairie Schooner, TriQuarterly*

The author wishes to thank Frank Bidart, Bob Hershon, Dick Lourie, Mark Pawlak, and Ron Schreiber for their comments and suggestions.

Cover art by Pamela Flint. Image suggested by a photograph taken by Hiroyuki Usami of the mausoleum of Chian Lin near Xi'an.

Library of Congress Cataloging-in-Publication Data
Jin, Ha
    Wreckage / Ha Jin.
        p. cm.
    ISBN 1-882413-98-9 (cloth) -- ISBN 1-882413-97-0 (pbk.)
        1. China--Poetry. I. Title.
    PS3560.I6 W74 2001
811'.54--dc21   00-050039

Produced at The Print Center, Inc. 225 Varick St., New York, NY 10014, a non-profit facility for literary and arts-related publications. (212) 206-8465

Contents

Prologue

"I came to explore the wreck.
The words are purposes.
The words are maps."

Adrienne Rich

The Cycle of the River

Yu the Great: a Legend

Soon the angry gods turned the Yellow Valley
into a swamp, where water and reeds
swelled toward the fumy sky,
serpents and crocodiles devouring people.
Yu's father stole some Divine Loam.
With it he stemmed the flood,
but the Fire God wrapped him in flames—
the water broke loose again.
Yu had to continue the struggle.

Hundreds of miles up, in the grasslands,
the river flowed clear and peaceful.
But entering the ocherous plain
it roared and rolled, poured silt
into the valley, and drowned our crops
and homes year after year.

Yu set out to survey the river.
He took a sled on mud, a boat on water,
a wagon on land, and trudged up
mountains with a spiked cane.

He divided the land into nine states,
linked them with solid roads,
dug waterways along the valley,
dammed the marshes that had overflowed.
Still the river could not be tamed.
It pranced around, shattering dikes.

For eight years Yu lived among
the laborers and never returned home
although three times he passed
his hovel and heard his children cry.

He realized the river was a divine animal
that would run tempestuous if bridled,
so he opened three mountains for
a new channel and widened waterways
to guide the water toward the ocean.

The river was calmed.
We had land to sow and populate—
villages emerged, then towns,
then cities, then a country.

Yu's deeds made him our king.
Thus began our first dynasty.

A Burial

We were pulling a bundle packed
with green branches and earth,
twenty feet across
and a hundred feet long.
We were to lodge it in place
to plug the holes burrowed
by foxes and badgers.

Singing in one voice, we sank
the bundle along the dike.
Immediately two boats loaded
with rocks were scuttled
against the bundle.

As the second boat was going down
it dragged Ah Shan into the water,
his legs caught by the gunnel.
He yelled, "Oh Mama, help!
Get me out, brothers!"

We tried
but couldn't pull him out.
Not daring to give the river time,
seven hundred men rushed over
to drop sacks of earth and rocks.

So—we buried him alive.
For days his voice
squeaked under our soles.

The dike was saved. Now
miles of stones cloak its surface,
but every April
Ah Shan's mother throws
dumplings into the river
and begs the fish not to eat her son.

Closing a Breach

Each spring our Emperor sent troops
to repair the breach at Gourd Bend.
Eight provinces had no harvest for years,
famine and plague thinning our
land, flooded or cracked by droughts.
Wolves fattened on corpses in the plain.

Again he arrived in October to offer
a sacrifice on the bank. He ordered
all the Royal Guards, even the generals,
to join the work—to carry wood, straw,
earth and rocks. We all took part,
sweating as though soaked in rain.

Still the water went on surging,
no way for us to close the gap.
Our Emperor was about to drop
into the river bleating lambs,
a jade camel, two plump girls,
a bushel of gold coins,
a pair of bronze quadripots—

so heartbroken he broke into song:
"Heavens, how can we piece together
the smashed Gourd?
So many provinces becoming ocean.
This water is drowning my people.
How can we drain it?
We have removed several hills,
where can we get more earth?
We have cut all the nearby woods,
how can we find more timber?
Winter's coming, everywhere
fish are swimming with ease,

but we men have to toil like
beasts of burden, without hope.
Mother River, have pity on us,
please return to your old course.
Now enjoy these small gifts.
We shall give you more."

Our tears falling into the torrents,
we too chanted the song.
The river seemed to relent
remaining calm for a month.
That was how we relocked the dam
and topped it with the Pity Pagoda.

A Change

The river gives no warning.
We were flailing sorghum that afternoon
when a man shouted from the road,
"The river's coming. Run for your lives!"

We scrambled up the hill while
the head of the water thundered past
tossing tables, bridges, roofs,
carriages, bodies, livestock.
A buffalo was mooing in the flood,
stuck to an elm with a plow,
then the animal disappeared in the waves
which were spinning pots, wheels,
pitchers, cauldrons, barrels, bins.

Around us people were howling,
their children had drowned
and their parents vanished.
Some prayed to heaven that the river
would spare their ancestors' graves;
some sat on the grass trembling,
assuring one another
they were lucky to be alive.

We thought the water would withdraw soon.
Week after week we waited
and paddled around to look for food.
Yesterday word came that the river
had shifted its course
and would keep our fields for good.

A Weapon

Under this lake (so sandy
that fish jump out to breathe)
once a town was thriving,
inhabited by several peoples—
Huns, Jurchens, Tobas, Hans, Mongols.
They basked in the frontier's freedom
and ignored the new dynasty.

The governor ordered its citizens
to surrender, but they refused.
They strangled the envoy,
roasted oxen and sheep,
drained wineskins, and poisoned
scimitars, arrows, spears.

One night the dam that stood above the town
was opened.
Torrents swept their homes down the lowland.
Within half an hour
the town disappeared.
A few men clung to treetops
calling to the army boats
for rescue—

One by one
we put them to the ax.

A Temple

In the morning sun, the bell lingers,
incense smoke surrounding
the statues and the bronze tablets
that record royal visits.
Monks are reciting sutras
beyond the mossy wall.

How many temples once
stood here before this one?
All were built for the same purpose—
to appease the river
and lock in the head of floods.

Through two thousand years
hundreds of herds of goats walked
down that coiled path,
each carrying a pair of glazed tiles
for the temples' roofs,
golden or green, all kept
under the sandy soil now.

The goats were sacrificed to the gods,
then eaten by stonecutters,
carpenters, masons, sculptors.
When a temple was raised
the Emperor would come to inscribe
its name, plant an evergreen tree,
promote thousands of officials.

So the construction continues.
We are told the river can be sated
even though every few decades here
it swallows a temple.

A Drought

What has become of the river
so determined to be our woe?
Last fall it flooded like an ocean
and took away our harvest,
but now in midsummer it yields
no water. For a whole month
its stream has been gone;
carts can cross the main channel,
in which sand has buried
fish, turtles, broken buckets.
Our fields are baked, barren and gray.
Water, water, where can we get water
for people, animals, seeds?

We're all starving, but have
no place to beg for food.
Our land is dying of thirst:
elms and willows stripped of bark,
grass gone, clouds dry like rock,
even mountains seem withered.
Some parents have eaten their children;
fresh graves are opened
for the flesh on the bones;
a dipper of cash cannot even
buy a dipper of grain;
peasants are rising up everywhere—
still the river withholds
its water.

Oh if only
a July flood would come!
although most sheepskin boats
have become food.

A Human Scarecrow

She holds a slingshot and a chive pie.
Beside her, on the straw mat,
sits a pile of pebbles, ready
to be shot at an intruder from
the sky. But for sparrows
she has a brass gong that
can flutter their chirrupy hearts.
To jays she will wave
her floral coat on the tip
of a bamboo pole.

Dazed by the sun
she gazes at the melon field,
her eyes bleared, like those
watching the water in the west.
By now she's used to the work,
too tired for tears.

This year the river is peaceful,
few bodies available
for crows, whose fortune
feeds on human calamities.
If a flock of them land here
this five-year-old will crawl
out of the tattered shade
to charge at the thieves with
her pole and her doleful voice.

Seized

Li Po chanted, "The Yellow River
comes from heaven
flowing east into the ocean
and will never return."
He was thinking of time
that has its own springs and waters.
Each of us is gathered in
a wave, which drifts or bounds,
then subsides, replaced by others.

Like the river
time has run its cycles
through human fervor and ruins.

Look at that sandy ribbon on the horizon,
like a piece of silk
flickering in the north wind.
That's the river, raised by our effort.
Caged in high dikes,
it flows easily above our city,
where factories bustle day and night,
where trains blow dark whistles.

Who can keep the river up
in the clouds forever?

Someday it will thunder down
like millions of crazed
elephants and whales.
So, many of us live as though
there were no tomorrow.

Fate

The river is our curse and our temperament.
It is a god, a twisted dragon that
struggles to reach the Pacific.

Up on the mountain stands Yu the Great
gazing at the coppery loops and curves,
his palm turned downward to soothe the turbulence

in the water and in our veins.
The sky is calm, the clouds motionless.
To have a peaceful year is fortunate

although from the moon you would see
the river, its back arched and tightened,
ready to leap again.

Words and Tongues

A Diviner's Confession

The King reads the cracks on
a burnt turtle shell for an oracle,
which he needs to decide on a battle,
or an alliance, or a sacrifice.
Whenever a plastron on charcoal
starts to crackle—pock pack puck,
the courtiers will fall face down
shaken by the turtle's voice.

Fools. They take the noise
as sacred words and never
consider these facts:

I choose a shell according to
the shape, size and density I want;
I scrape and polish the shell
and drill hollows on it
at any spots I think proper;
I apply a red-hot poker to the hollows
in a flexible order.
I make the cracks appear
horizontal or vertical, traverse
or halfway, straight or curved.
I manufacture divine messages.

(What's hard to guess
is the sovereign heart that
glooms or storms without a cloud.)

In Confucius's Class

Master, eight days after you became
the Police Chief of Lu State
you had Shao-zheng beheaded.
You've taught us never to do to others
what you won't have them do to you.
Why did you not bestow benevolence on him?

(I dare not be more specific.
Last summer Shao-zheng and the Master
lectured at the same hour.
Three times in a row people went to
his talk and gave us an empty hall.)

That's a good question, young man.
Bear in mind that a well-ordered state
should winnow out five kinds of people:
those who have acute, dangerous minds,
those who behave peculiarly
but refuse to reform themselves,
those who utter false words
and strive to justify them,
those who write strange books
full of recondite allusions,
those who follow evil, thriving on it.

Tell me, which one of the five kinds
did Shao-zheng not belong to?
Did he not deserve his end?
Stopping a man like him
will help our Tao prevail.

(They left his headless body
on the terrace before
the Security Bureau for three days
to feed rooks and warn wicked people.)

The Script

So the wars went on for another century.
Under heaven roads sprang up, unconnected,
from three to eight feet wide,
impossible for vehicles to travel;
forms of money also ran wild—
precious stones, shells, silk, bones;
scholars were busy inventing bizarre words
while people followed their own tongues
writing scripts of Worm,
of Vine, of Fish, of Cloud, of Bird.

As soon as the First Emperor conquered
the other kingdoms, he set standards
for coinage, roads, weights and measures.
His ministers advised him to fix
written words, which they argued
form a foundation for the Empire
because a disordered official script
would cloud meanings, causing chaos.

The High Minister designed a script called
the Clerk Style, whose characters looked
august and simple, so his dictionary
of thirty-three thousand words
was carved on stone tablets while
all the other scripts were banned.
Misinscribers were caught and sent away
to build canals or the Great Wall
after their faces were cut or seared.

So today we write the same script
that is atemporal—a stone lyre
among the chorus of living tongues.
It has bound us together, synchronizing
our songs and shrieks, and kept hundreds
of dialects noteless on the page.

An Exile's Song

Skylarks are destined to fly away
while sparrows infest the ground.
Orchids and chrysanthemums fall
before a hand picks them.
How true is the ancient saying:
the world enjoys muck and stench.

When the sun and moon are misplaced,
when time is shaped by wicked words
to suit a wanton will, when
loyalty only breaks loyal hearts,
I shall float away with the wind.

*

From this cliff I gaze at the north.
The familiar clouds are prancing
like animals on the skyline.
When can I head for my homeland?
Birds have crossed the sea
but will return to their old nests;
foxes, when dying, point their heads
toward the hills of their holes.

Oh if only I could subdue
my gregarious soul, which
flies home on windy nights.

Burying Them

At last our Emperor gave the orders—we began
to confiscate books and round up scholars
who had slandered the royal family
using ancient stories to mock the present.

All books throughout the Empire had to be surrendered
to officials within a month, except those
on agriculture, divination, and medicine.
Disobeyers would have their clans erased.

About five hundred scholars were taken
to Bliss Hall to be tried by the ministers
who matched them in learning and eloquence.
Our swords were gleaming in the sunlight

that poured in through the open windows.
How pasty their faces suddenly turned.
They pointed fingers at one another
and tried every trick to save their own skins;

some pissed and shit in their robes,
one stopped breathing before his trial.
Thank heaven for divine retribution!
We hauled out over four hundred of them

to be dumped into a common grave.
We had fun, slapping and spanking them
with our swords before we pushed them in.
Of what use now were their clever tongues?

And where were their headfuls of knowledge?
Under our shovels, in the smoke of books,
they screamed Mother and called us Brothers,
but no words could deter the cascades of dirt.

Words by a Castrated Writer

After I complete this book
I shall keep it in the Mount of Fame
so that it reaches people
who will chew my words in their sleep.

I'll be remembered not as a fool who lost
his testicles to the Emperor's anger
but as a man who chose emasculation
over a noose for the sake of his work.

How I would regret it if I were gone
without seeing my thoughts
carved in words, without making sure
my bitterness will stir posterity.

A human being has only one death,
which may weigh less than a feather
or more than a mountain—
it depends on how death is used.

Therefore I won't die a useless death
to gladden a few scoundrels.
Let those at court ridicule me as they like.
For them I'm "a mere servant in the harem."

Someday my headstone will say:
Although he left no heir
He produced a great book
That fathered several styles.

The Mount of Fame is the royal library.

Between a Lamb and a Dog

The new Emperor was merely eight,
ruling our country with birds,
crickets, butterflies, grasshoppers.

His Prime Minister, an author
of two books, planned to start
his own dynasty, but feared
the court might not cooperate,
so he gave a test.

In Meridian Hall
he presented a lamb to the Emperor,
saying, "Here's a foreign dog."

"You are wrong," said the boy.
"He doesn't bow-wow or bite.
He's not a dog but a lamb.
Little lamb, how old are you?"

"If Your Majesty doesn't believe me,
please ask your servants here."

Asked, most of the courtiers bit
their tongues. A few claimed
indeed it was a dog, but two said
it looked like an Arabian lamb
(if only the creature had bleated).

The Prime Minister went home
and told his son-in-law:
"Let both lamb-men be dog feed."

A Court Proposal

For centuries our Empire has been harassed
by the barbarians, who can leave home with ease
and swiftly penetrate our frontier defenses.
Why so? One obvious reason is that
there are no pretty women in the North.
So their men are tough and fierce.

Your Majesty, I propose we let them
have thousands of beauties.
These women will fix the savages
to their land—the men will be ensnared
and befuddled by feminine charm,
averse to the life on horseback.

We should teach their women footbinding
and open clothing shops in the prairie.
Gradually the men will learn to prize
feminine beauty—the willow waist,
the lily face, the lotus gait—
which will soften their harsh natures.

Thus their descendants will be civilized,
fond of books and shy of the spear.
Within three generations
they will belong to us.

The First Brush

In his dream he saw the sky open,
a vast piece of paper in the air,
and he wielded a brush like a rafter
to inscribe words among the clouds.
Sunlight gleamed through the lines
that wavered with herons and pelicans.
The words he had written
were breaking into lilies;
now and then he rinsed his brush
in the Celestial Lake.

Waking up, he decided to stop seeing
the girls at the pleasure house;
instead he would devote himself
to classics, poetry, calligraphy,
to realize the promise
just revealed by heaven.
He also considered entering a temple
or a monastery, if necessary;
life, after all, was brief
while writing could be immortal.
He wouldn't mind resigning
his paltry position at the palace.

At sunset drums and pipes
burst into his cottage—
the Emperor having just passed away,
the prince was summoning him to court
to compose the obituary
and the funeral oration,
to write records, messages,
lists, invitations, decrees.
His parents cried joyfully
while their neighbors smiled
with green faces.

It was this moment scholars would kill for,
to become the country's First Brush,
a post he would hold for thirty years.

Reproach

My letter warned you not to go
—the war was merciless, the road
to the fleeing court equally difficult.
But bewitched, you set out
and left your wife and children behind.

Heaven knows how they get by—
perhaps starving, at night
trembling under a broken roof.

True, our duty is to serve the country,
but you, what can you do?
Can you wield a sword or lead troops?
Can you wave a banner or blow a bugle?

See, how easily the rebels
caught you and brought you here
to smell burned animals
and taste their barbaric music.

*

Five months ago we were besieged,
outside the city wall
the rebel army ready to charge in,
inside, our troops mounting defense.

Then the Emperor changed his mind—
the entire court fled toward Szechwan
leaving us civilians to defend Chang An.

How could we fight a quarter million
cavalry and swordsmen!
Just in one day the capital fell—
killing, screaming everywhere,
smoke blocking out daylight.

*

Now that you are in this trap
you'd better take it easy.
For the time being we are safe
(I gave a singing girl
to a rebel general).

But don't stroll on the streets
with your neck so straight.
Don't wear your official cap—
allegiance to the court is a crime.
Don't chant in the park.
Some barbarians understand your words
and will behead you for that.
Don't try to escape—
if they catch you, you'll be a goner.
Don't cry after drinking.
Many people are more miserable
than you and I.

Yesterday
after hearing you recite your poems
Lu Ben, the herbalist, took to his bed
saying he missed home.
He lost his only child last fall.

The country is broken,
but mountains and rivers remain.
Spring is here again,
cherries and apricots blooming.
Look, under the charred eaves
swallows are rebuilding their nests,
dragonflies flitting with skinny wings.

A Lost Scholar

At the crossroads he looks for a sign,
but finds none. Swallows
are passing, up and down—
up and down—in the spring air.
He sits on a boulder waiting
for someone to break the skyline.

His donkey brays, kicks the dust
and shakes the heavy load
of classics on its back.
Tears glaze his eyes while
dusk nibbles the trails,
katydids hissing a labyrinth.

How could a human being travel
without a map or a destination
like a fish in the ocean
or a leaf in the wind?

For the first time he is crushed
by the weight of free choice.

Metal and Flesh

The Worthy Ruler's Way

After Han Feizi [313?-230? B.C.]

When overwhelmed with right and wrong
you must remain godlike,
blank-faced, empty and still,
and sit in darkness to observe the light.
You must not show preference or desire,
otherwise your ministers will know how
to please you, hiding their true colors,
ready to invade your rights.
You are so empty that your mind
seems to dwell nowhere,
unfathomable like the Tao itself.
You stay so still that you see
but don't appear to notice a thing
and you listen but seem to give no ear.
Yet your presence is constant—
your ministers tremble before you
as you take credit for all accomplishments
while they take blame for any mistake.

In your right hand you carry Favor,
in your left hand Punishment.
When you grant rewards
they should fall like seasonable rain,
nourishing, benign, and moderate,
but your punishments must seem summary,
like lightning indifferent to
a temple or an animal or a tree.
Wielding this pair of tools
to control your ministers,
you need to do nothing else.
Without your speaking a word, they will
produce suitable answers and plans;

you remain idle, yet good works will multiply
and all affairs reach settlement.

So be like heaven, be like earth,
but never feel attached to anyone.

Human Pig

Later the Emperor promised to crown
the son of his favorite concubine
but the court opposed him—
he had to swallow his words.

As soon as he died
the Empress had the concubine seized.
They chopped off her hands,
gouged out her eyes, seared her earholes,
stuffed her with herbs to take
away her voice, then
dumped her into an outhouse
(whose lintel still shows the words
Human Pig, engraved on stone).

The Empress often led her guests to
the pigpen. They'd empty
their bowels and bladders in there.
Sometimes a flagon tipped,
wine trickled through a hole—
burbling on the smacking lips.

A Sewing Song

Hard, hard are our men's hearts.
The best of them fall
on the battleground, ashamed
to be held back by women's arms.
They say, "A real man should
be buried in a green hill
or return home wrapped
in a horse's hide."

Have they not seen grass pierce
skulls in the plain?
White skulls, thousands of them,
still dream of the days
as a happy bridegroom.
Don't they know a general's fame
grows in the soil of human bones?
Doesn't the blood in the wind
dampen their battle drums?
Who has ever heard
the dead can come back home?

Cold, cold are our scissors,
but we won't stop sewing tonight.
The royal inspector is leaving
tomorrow morning, so
let us hope these robes
will reach the border soon,
before ice and snow.

Lord of Heaven, please help
our Emperor remove the Tartars
even though his orders have
toughened so many leathery hearts.

Lament

After Cai Yan (2nd century A.D.)

1

From the north came the Huns,
their swords and armor flashing.
Wherever they reached,
towns and cities were razed,
bodies scattered on roadsides,
vultures cawing and flapping like clouds.
On their horses' flanks hung men's heads;
behind their horses followed carts
loaded with women and girls.
They headed inland
where roads were more mountainous.

I looked around feeling my stomach ruptured.
There were thousands of us,
mothers and daughters separated;
no one dared to talk or cry.
My maid had been butchered the night before
because she sobbed—too terrified
to entertain the soldiers.
Wrapped in a blanket, I begged heaven,
"Please let me join her!"

2

The prairie differs from our plain.
Their customs are crude,
nobody cares about good manners.
They respect the strong
and despise the weak and old.
Sheep and cattle swarm around their yurts,
so many of them that the herds
look like hornets and ants.

A chieftain had me summoned to his chamber
and later made me his ninth wife.
I was always half starved,
unable to eat foul cheese and raw meat.
At night I heard the Yangtze murmuring;
in the morning I watched the clouds
drifting toward the Great Wall.
Sometimes I followed them,
winds throwing my robe up
and shrieking in my ears.

Whenever a visitor came from the south
I'd rush to him, but he'd know
little about my hometown.
Although I had two sons with the chieftain
I missed my parents—
if I couldn't return alive
I wanted to be buried
in our family's graveyard.

3

Then the two countries stopped fighting.
Our Emperor had pity on my father who
had passed away, and he sent over
jade and gold to ransom me.
Hearing the news, I burst into tears.
All the inland women said
I was fortunate, the only one
who could return. They envied me.

But freedom meant I had to abandon my children
who were too little to understand.
They held my neck and cried,
"Where are you going, Mama?
Is it true you're leaving?
Will you come back?
You were always kind to us,

why did you change suddenly?
We're still young and we need you."

Their words threw me into a trance
as though my heart had stopped.
I embraced them and together we were wailing.
The horses, stunned, wouldn't move,
the wheels sinking into the mud.
All the spectators were sighing
while the dew on the road
flickered like a river of tears.

The way home was a thousand miles long,
too short compared with my love
for my children, who enter
my wordless dreams night after night.

4

My mother has disappeared.
Our hometown no longer exists.
Everywhere are white bones,
houses and temples leveled in the grass.

Where is home?

Accompanied by my shadow
I walk along the mossy streets
that have no human sounds.
Only wolves cry in the distance.

I climb up the mountain.
At the summit my soul seems
to be flying away.

How slow this life is!
Can it ever shed grief?

A Return

Finally we can go home—after
five years on the front
longing for the way eastward.
The cold rain is soaking our bones,
but our hearts can hardly hold
the happiness. Yes, happy
for having shed our uniforms,
happy for being alive.

When I left you, my hair was dark,
now it's gray and sparse.
How war and grief can age a man!
How often I saw you cry in my dreams,
your apron tumbling in a wind.

Are watermelons from our garden
still large and sweet?
Do you still keep the parakeet who
had smooth feathers but a wooden tongue?
I heard deer had trampled
our fields, burrowed by worms.

My heart is shaking and my legs weary
as the way home shortens.
Do you still await this man—
your two-night bridegroom?

The Expatriates

The news threw them into tears:
the foreign troops have crossed the river
and burned down the capital;
no army moved to stop them,
every general and governor
defending his own territory;
the prince fell to an arrow
and the court surrendered—
their country became a memory.

Now they remember the lesson
their master taught them long ago:
"Your country is a nest while
you are all eggs in it—
if the nest is overturned
no egg will remain unbroken."

For twelve years they have
gone from land to land—
scholars and artisans
dreaming of home, lamenting
their fate, waiting to return.

Now the nest is gone,
but few of them are broken,
all stunned by the prospect that
some eggs will have to hatch
in the elements.

Betrayal

Come, you can't forget those days
when the foreign rebels surrounded us.
There was no food left in the town.
Parents exchanged their babies—
to have them at other homes
bathed, killed, cooked and eaten.
When someone died of hunger or disease
people would rush over
to cut him up for meat.

Our starved troops were losing their morale,
so you had me dragged out. I still hear
you speak to the officers and soldiers:
"You all defend this city with
one heart for our Emperor.
I cannot offer you my limbs to eat
because I have to lead the defense,
but I dare not keep this woman.
Please have her."

Have you forgotten what I said?—
"I'm still useful although
I'm merely a concubine.
Unlike your wife, I can read to you
and copy your writings.
Remember how I pleased you."

Some of the men seemed uncomfortable
whispering that I was too young
and too pretty for the blade.
But you gave orders—
they took me apart.

Afterward they began butchering
girls and women; then boys
and old men ended up in kitchen pots.
My father too became a meal.
By the time the imperial army came to
break the siege, how many people had gone
through their countrymen's bowels?
Over four thousand. Even
the rebels might not have killed so many.

The Emperor promoted you to court
and awarded you a two-page biography
in the *Royal Records of Loyal Men,*
yet I'll never recant my words
that inflamed your mind
and cost me my flesh:
"You ought to surrender
so as to save the civilians.
To be human, we may have to face
the charge of betraying our country."

Surrender

When most towns near Nanking had fallen to
the Manchu cavalry, the Chinese commander
defending the city offered to capitulate.
The enemy ordered him to sign a surrender
at their camp, but he must not
bring along more than one guard.
From hundreds of soldiers he picked a man
who had followed him through many battles.
Together they set out along the Yangtze
with a furled banner on the guard's waist.

But halfway there the soldier
was possessed by a spirit.
He stopped his horse and began
to curse the general, calling him
a traitor, a shameless pig,
even declared all his children
would become national criminals
hated by millions.
A wasp buzzed on the shoulder of
the general as he barked orders,
but the soldier wouldn't shut up
and cursed louder and louder

till he got off his horse and plunged
into an eddy, still shouting,
"I'll never surrender.
Let me die a Chinese ghost!"
As though the river cared
about the nationality of a corpse.

On the Great Wall

1

We are climbing the Great Wall
that goes along the mountain chain
turning, twining, rolling east
toward the bay of the Yellow Sea.
In the north, wisps of smoke wavering,
beyond the horizon is the Mongolian Plain.
When winds blow in spring, dust drifts
across the land and over the wall
flying south to the cities inland.
It's autumn now—maples flame the hills
and torch the passing clouds.

Our guide, a slender young woman, tells us
this is the largest construction of mankind,
the only man-made object that
astronauts can see from the moon.
It's a project that took thirteen centuries
and spread fifteen hundred miles
across northern China. She says,
"The Great Wall proves the diligence,
wisdom and love for peace of the Chinese
because it was built only for defense."

On a terrace children are dancing,
brandishing whips to urge imaginary horses.
Below the mountain parasols are blooming;
bells and vendors' cries
mingle with the smell of roasted lamb.
Peace seems to have been here for a millennium.

2

The Mongols arrived,
every man riding eight horses

carrying two bows and a leather shield.
After conquering half of Europe, Genghis Khan
had remembered the South, where
waters were beautiful as in a painting,
temples and mansions sloping up to heaven.
He craved comfort and longevity,
tired of raiding and ruling on horseback.

The Mongols didn't touch these battlements.
With gold they bribed a guard
so a gate opened at night—
their horses burst in like a torrent.

But they had to conquer the empire
village by village, town by town,
city by city, province by province.
It took them two generations to trap
the last prince, drown his troops
and court in the ocean, and turn
paddy fields to pastureland.

3

All sing praises of the Great Wall,
but no one mentions the skeletons
under the bricks, rocks, ramparts, roads.

Listen carefully, the ancient work songs
still lingering, full of sweat and misery,
women's shrieks sharp as cicadas,
wheels squeaking, men moaning—
all are ringing in the wind.

The wind is the same
although the land has changed hands.
Shame and glory have been the sovereigns' tale.

Bound

A Sculpture of Lovers (circa 200 A.D.)

A moment stolen turned eternal.
They sat against a blossoming wall,
her arm around his neck,
he embraced her shoulders,
his fingers touching her nipple.
As their mouths joined,
the bulky shadow of his nose
fell on her cheek, soon
eclipsed by her hair.
She moaned, "Hold me, tighter!"

From the other side of the wall
their matron called
and ordered them to put a stove
into the guest room,
but they could no longer be summoned,
beyond curses and canes.

Together they stayed
in the sunset and moonshine,
saturated with the elements
and radiating silence—
an unknown chisel
gathered them into stone.

To Her Sister

Chickens, ducks and pigeons still
goose-step in our front yard—
in a moment I will gather them
into their coops for the night.
Our hemp and fruit trees
reach the crown of the northern hill.
Why can't you support my choice?
What else do I need
besides food and peace?

The red willows and the green shoals
are the same every year,
and only the brook shifted
a little last spring.
This is the place where
I will raise my children.
Please don't mention again
that gentleman who travels
from province to province.

Afterward I Became a Model Wife

He got off his black horse at the roadside
and observed me picking
mulberry leaves for silkworms.

I was aware of his eyes
fierce as a leopard's,
but I pretended not to see him.

"How do you do?" He came over.
As I turned around
my breath almost stopped.

How could I ignore such a man,
husky and regal, apparently
an official or an officer in disguise?

(My husband had left three days
after we were married
to hold a post in Han State.

For seven years
I had lived like a widow
without a word from him.)

The man came closer and patted
my shoulder, then held
the end of my silk girdle.

"Please let me go," I moaned
afraid he'd pull
to loosen my skirt.

"No, I won't." He smiled.
"I saw you from the top of the mountain.
You looked like a large swan."

He took out a few pieces of silver
and dropped them into
my basket hanging on a branch.

"I'll come to see you
tomorrow afternoon," he said.
"Please wait for me here."

He mounted his horse and galloped away.
Somehow he looked familiar
but I wasn't sure if I had met him.

Without delay I gathered my things
and went back to the village
planning to stay home the next day.

But at my front gate I saw
the black horse tethered to the willow
planted by my husband.

A swoon swept me down as I realized
that man was my own. How could I enter
the home that was no longer the same?

I left my bracelets in the basket,
rose to my feet and ran away
toward the swamp in the woods.

A Childless Merchant

I put on a dappled cape and carry
a tureen of turtle soup to their home.
A fifty-year-old, I grovel at

my parents' feet and cry like a baby
to make them happy.
But they don't think I'm funny,

so I begin to play horse
riding a bamboo chair in the yard
and chanting "My Papa Is a Shiny Bull."

Mother slaps me, claiming the soup
is too bland (her taste buds are gone).
I'm stunned, then burst into sobs.

She says, "You never cried
when I whacked you before,
why sniveling like this?"

"Mommy, your hand used to hurt,
but now I don't feel a scratch.
I'm so sad you are old."

Father says, "That's why
we want a grandson. Rice Bag,
when can you give us one?"

(If only I dared to spit
in his face, red and hairy
like a monkey's ass!)

Cleansing the Body

After two bowls of yellow wine
I was drunk, soft like mud.
Father and Uncle stripped off my pants,
tied me to a table,
and rubbed some balm on my privates.
With an ox-ear knife, at one stroke
Father cut off my dick and nuts.
I screamed, but lost my voice,
my heart throbbing in my throat,
my limbs contracting, my hands
wet with blood. If only I had died!

While fainting I heard Father say,
"Get the oil ready, quick."
In the kitchen our red hen was cackling.
She had just laid another twin-yolked egg.

They inserted a goose quill
into my urethra so that I could pee.
For a whole month I lay on my back
like having a broken spine,
my hips on coal ashes and earth
that they changed for me every other day.
Pepper, white wax, sesame oil
were applied to my wound
to make it fester a little
so that new flesh could grow.
Every time they redressed my groin
I'd gasp and groan, writhing
between life and death.
For the first hundred days
no scab was allowed to form,
not until the wound almost healed.

Father had fried my genitals,
wrapped them in a piece of wax paper,
and put them in a lacquered box
which sits on a beam in our roof.
That's his way to wish
for my rise at court.

Last week a senior eunuch said
my nine-year-old privates
could join me only in my grave.

A Young Girl's Lament

In the first moon of my seventh year
my earlobes were pierced for gold rings.
I was told a girl had to suffer twice—
having her ears pierced and her feet bound.
My binding began in the third moon
after Mother asked an old man for an auspicious day.
I wept and hid in a neighbor's house,
but Mother found me and dragged me home.
She shut our door, boiled water
and took out scissors, binding cloths,
bowed shoes, a knife, needles and thread.
I begged her to postpone for another week,
but she said, "Today's a lucky day.
If bound now, your feet will never hurt."

She bathed my feet, put them on a stool,
sprinkled alum, and cut the nails.
Then she bent my toes toward the sole
and tied them with a cloth twelve
feet long and two inches wide—
first she did my right foot, then my left.
I was soaked in sweat and tears
but dared not make any noise
biting a brush to suppress my screams.
She told me, "With lotus feet
you'll marry a nice man. You know
we're not rich and you have an ordinary face,
so I'm giving you a second chance."

Done with the binding, she ordered me to walk.
When I did, I fell on the floor,
my feet, my feet no longer my own!

That night Mother wouldn't let me remove the shoes.
My feet felt on fire and I couldn't sleep.
The next day I got into a haystack
but was found and forced to walk.
From then on beatings and curses
became a part of my life whenever
I loosened the wrappings in secret.

Four months later all my toes
were pressed against the soles except
my big toes, which were bound too,
the narrow cloths forcing them upward
into the shape of an old moon.
Whenever I ate fish or freshly killed meat
my feet would swell and pus would drip.
Mother scolded me for putting my weight
on my heels when I walked, saying
my feet would never have a pretty shape.
She'd remove my bindings and wipe the pus
and repeat that only with the loss of flesh
could my feet grow small and slim.
If I pricked a sore by mistake
blood would trickle like a stream.

Every two weeks I changed to new shoes.
Each pair was a fifth of an inch smaller
than the previous one. It took pressure
to get into the unyielding shoes.
I wanted to stay in bed, but Mother
always made me move around.
After changing a dozen pairs
my feet were reduced to three inches.

Then my younger sister began her binding.
When no one was around we'd weep together.
In summer my feet smell like a chicken coop;
in winter they are icy cold for lack
of circulation. On each foot

the toes curl in like dead caterpillars.
Who would think they belong to a human being?
My toenails press the flesh
like scabs, and the folded soles
cannot be soothed when they ache
or scratched when they itch.
My shanks are thin, my feet humped,
ugly, rotten, clumsy, useless.
If only I had my maid's large feet!

To Survive

That muddy summer the plague came.
Half the village died in three months.
When my brother's belly bulged out
Father told him to go to some temples
to collect magic ash.
He went to those nearby,
but the ash didn't shrink him
and only blackened his tongue.

Father heard about a doctor
in the county town who,
if paid enough cash,
would draw off the stomach water
to cure the disease.
So he sold all our land
and carried my brother to him
dragging me along as I was
too young to be left alone.

The doctor had a white beard,
a ruddy face and a flat nose.
There was a glowing brazier in his room
with an iron skewer buried in the coals
that crackled like peas.
He kneaded my brother beneath
the ribs, saying, "His spleen has
grown eyes, I'm going to blind them."

After mumbling some scripture
he pulled out the red-hot skewer,
stabbed it into my brother's stomach
and twisted it several times.
My brother screamed, then blacked out,
water flowing on the floor.

The air smelled of burned flesh.
I bawled and thought he was dead,
but the doctor said he was fine,
the evil eyes now seared.

Father carried him home,
flies following us all the way.

My brother groaned for a few days
unable to eat anything.
Soon his belly turned clammy
filled with pus and blood.
He died within a month.

Then Father grew weak.
Before he passed away he took me to a temple,
whose clay god is called Gao Mang.
He begged the god to adopt me,
changed my name to Gao
and left me with the monks.

Among our clan of seven families
two little girls are also alive, serving
as child wives in a northern province.

A Contract

On the thirteenth day of the first moon,
in the seventh year of Forever Peace,
the carpenter Tao Long from Stone Village,
short of grain and unable to
procure it by any other means,
sells his son Cheng-min to his cousin,
the landowner Liu Peng in Swallow Town.
The price is set at 200 bushels of rice
with the option of repurchase.
Once the sale is clinched, there will be
no interest on the provided grain
and no pay for Cheng-min's labor.
The earliest time for repurchasing him
will be the beginning of the sixth year,
but his owner retains the right
to price him according to his new worth.
If Cheng-min injures himself or falls ill
or dies during the first five years,
his brother Cheng-shan will take his place
or his father will return the rice
(commensurate with the remaining time).
If he steals anything from a third person,
either in the country or in town,
he himself will make the reparation.
If he damages anything belonging to his buyer
he will compensate him by extra work.

This contract, signed
in the presence of both parties,
demonstrates our mutual agreement.

On Issuing a Residential Certificate

This piece of paper with the seal on it
shows you are a law-abiding citizen.
Whenever a stranger appears in your neighborhood
you must report him to us.
If a neighbor of yours commits a crime
you must turn him in, or you'll be punished
as an accomplice—either jailed
or sent away to build roads,
at the least you'll lose a finger or an ear.
But if you inform on him, you'll be rewarded
like a soldier who killed an enemy.

Bear in mind you should not have a large family,
which would be hard for us to supervise.
Any household with more than two grown sons
will be taxed twice over.
At peace you work your fields and provide
labor whenever our Emperor needs it;
when a war breaks out, by duty
you are a warrior and must fight with valor—
that's your chance for nobility.
Also, you're not allowed to travel.
If you have to go somewhere, such as
to a funeral or on a pilgrimage,
you must carry this certificate with you
and register wherever you stay.

In brief, with this piece of paper in hand
you and your four acres now own each other.

A Sedan Chair

The splendor of his governance
rests upon the peasants' bent shoulders.
Thirty-six men are panting
under bamboo poles, on which
his sedan chair is swaying.

Who would call this a chair?
It's a three-room vehicle—
he and his wife are napping in the chamber
while two maids, just relieved of fans,
lounge in another room.
In the front parlor a pug dog lies against
a legless table encircled by drum stools,
gossamer curtains soften the breeze,
a carpet of finches flutters
along with the bearers' feet
that often falter but always rhyme.
Outside, the roof sparkles as
golden tassels sprinkle shadows
on the veined backs and the conical hats.
A squadron of musketeers follows them,
the iron hooves thumping a fog of dust.

Along the street carriages halt
and pedestrians step aside—all watch
the governor heading for his uncle's
to see his second nephew leave
for the Martial Contest in the capital.

Ode on the Cangue

Sublime collar, divine wood and iron,
you have no desire for our flesh.
Your board and chain around a neck
remind us how unconditional
order and propriety must be.
If you pin one of us to the ground
you do it without brute force
but with the patience
of water raising grass.

How mercilessly you can keep
an offender's hands from reaching his face
as it turns into a playing field
for maggots. How you can reduce
a titan to a mere dependent on
anyone who might thrust
a scrap of food into his mouth
or lift a water ladle to his lips.
How you can barb tongues,
wet eyes, and raise goose
bumps on millions of hearts.

Master Teacher, Guardian of Virtue,
you have taught us the elegance
of bent spines and trembling knees.
Even our ova and sperm have learned
how to produce docile children,
let alone our souls, always
ready to embrace communal grace.

A cangue is a portable pillory.

Between Heaven and Earth

Questions

After lay Buddhist Aina

Lord of Heaven, how old are you?
Why have you no eye or ear
for our troubles?
Where's your forked grumble?

Those who kill, steal and bully others
bask in honor and security.
Those who follow your scriptures
are cold, starved, trampled.

Lord of Heaven, how can you govern
the earth like a fool
and let officials multiply
more than laborers and taxpayers?

Better if you were not there.
What a useless scarecrow you have
become, that rots in evil winds.
Why don't you topple down?

A Query

1

Hard as he tries, he cannot shake
his father from his mind.
The old man arrived last night
when the wind was sweet
swaying the window curtain
like a familiar robe.
Again the bearded mouth emerged
whimpering the same complaint—

his stay underground is not
uncomfortable, but he's lonesome;
the company of spirits bores him
because most of them speak
incomprehensible tongues
and some are deaf-mute.

2

After class he doesn't leave
and asks about the underworld.
His master says, "You don't understand
people yet, why worry about ghosts?"
A puff of wind lifts a curled leaf
that's swirling above
a book made of bamboo slips.

Still he's eager to see
if pain can catch a fleshless shape.
His master says, "I don't know enough
about life to think of death."

He withdraws, remembering
that our religion comprehends only man.

Reward and Punishment

After a sacrifice on top of Mount Tai
our Emperor turned back
descending the zigzag stone steps.
A storm came and he took shelter
under a juniper at the edge of a cliff.
Few drops of rain fell on him—
he was so pleased that he bestowed
on the tree an office of the third rank.

But his return trip was delayed at
a river by a torrential shower.
His retinue was soaked like molting birds.
A priest claimed a goddess living nearby
was to blame, so His Majesty
dispatched an army to cut down
all the trees on her mountain.

How outrageous she was, to forget
deities are appointed by man.

Equality

Like the armor of the rebel troops
who entered our capital after
defeating the royal army, chrysanthemums
have cloaked the city in gold.
Their scent drenches every street,
but their petals are frosted,
too dull to fetch the butterflies
that are all gone, frozen in grass.

How unfair it is that chrysanthemum
blooms when other flowers have fallen.
The rebel commander vows
that someday when he becomes a god,
he will rewrite the rules of nature
to make this flower unfold
together with apple blossoms.

Salvation

Earthly creatures, we all strive
to realize salvation through
prolonging our bodily existence:
the old practice tai chi
or martial arts in the morning;
the weak pray to all kinds of gods
for help against misfortune and illness;
the gentry eat anything with legs
(except for chairs and tables)
which can nourish muscles and brains—
they even relish human flesh
served in restaurants under
the name Two-Legged Lamb;
holy men never stop their breathing exercises,
some having abstained from sex for life;
hermits hide in mountains for
clean water, fresh air, and the company
of cranes—they advise young men,
who study the knack of longevity,
that if you have to marry,
do not take a beautiful wife;
as for our Queen, she still
dreams of the First Emperor
who dispatched a thousand virgin
boys and girls to the Blessed Isles,
which are said to lie somewhere in the east,
to search for herbs of immortality
(those fortunate children
never returned to this swamp of flesh;
legend has it that their blood
enriches a foreign race).

A Dragon Lover

He wrote a book about divine animals
and would play a dragon in a dance.
Though wingless, he studied how
to plow the clouds and mount the wind.

Atop his stable perched a dragon,
a weather vane, whose tail kept
beckoning the pair engraved
on the marble pillar in his porch.

In his bedroom dragons were welcome,
one glazed in a washbasin,
two entwined on the mosquito net,
saber teeth ablaze on a lampshade.

At last his name reached heaven.
A dragon came down to visit him.
As its scaly head nudged his door
ajar—he jumped out the window
yelling "Monster!"

A Sorcerer

When the slave arrived as
a tributary article from a vassal state,
a puny man who claimed to know magic—
my father was incredulous, having seen
many holy men, magicians, monks.
The slave said he often went to the ocean
to meet with goddesses and gods.
In his own words, "If Your Majesty
believes me, I shall turn all metals
to gold, all the breaches along
the Yellow River will close soon,
you will befriend many deities
and get the elixir of immortality."

My father ordered him to show us his power.
The slave placed chess pieces on a board
and shouted "Fight!" At once
the horses, elephants, chariots began
engaging one another, then the cannons
and soldiers all joined the battle.
Beyond the window a peacock burst out
squalling, raising its coined tail.
Amazed, my father conferred on him
the post of Five-Benefit General.

(For many years my father had been upset
by endless floods, the Mongols,
stubborn base metals, his aging face.)

Within a month the man was given
the titles of another three generals—
of Heaven, Earth, and the Great Way.
He was named Bliss Marquis and provided
with a wooded palace, twenty cartloads

of gold, a thousand slaves.
Eager to break into the divine world,
my father had an ivory seal carved for him
which carried these words—"Avenue to Heaven."
He wished to be a god soon, or at least
remain the sovereign of earth for good.

Three months passed, still the man
had done nothing. Desperate,
my father married one of my sisters to him.
Every night the bastard sneaked out,
saying he was going to the seashore to negotiate
with deities, or to some sacred mountain
to refine his elixir in a flaming cave.
Actually he went to teahouses, bath parlors, restaurants,
theaters, brothels, flower boats.
He was an idiot, toying with
the dragon's whiskers, and had no idea
that some eyes always followed him.

Last night when the moon blazed
into a blade, we ambushed him.
Now his head hangs above the city gate
with a hook through his nose and mouth,
though another sister of mine
is widowed in her early teens.

The Returned Crane

1

Then I land on the belfry.
A few arrows swish by and I cry,
"This is Ding Wei, back
from Cloud Mountain.
Please don't shoot!"

They hear me but they laugh.
Boys brandish slingshots—
pebbles ricochet and set
the bell tinkling in the wind.
I have to take wing.

The town hasn't changed much—
there are more trees,
the moat flashes like fish,
towers circled by smoke.

Why are the people so different,
so mean, so barbarous?

2

My clan clumps like a nest
of fledglings in the vast graveyard.
At last I find my parents—
they lie together in one grave,
whose stone says they missed me.

I fly about to see more.
Oh here's my little brother.
And his wife? Around them
nestle the mounds of
their children and grandchildren.

My heart outweighs my wings.
When I left with Master
for the mountain
I was told I'd lose nothing
but my human flesh.

A Gentleman's Dream

Dead drunk, he snores
like a bellows under the linden.
He dreams of a country
where the air is redolent of persimmon
and the sky shimmers with wings.

Amazed by such a giant,
Ant Emperor picks him as his son-in-law,
awards him a timbered palace,
an army of infantry, a brigade of sappers
and the dukedom of Wicker State.
The teenage princess bursts
into tears, waving goodbye
to her siblings, but in a trice
she becomes his corpulent duchess,
a mother of eight daughters and five sons
who are all healthy and handsome.

Wicker State has basked in his wisdom—
no door needs a bolt or a lock;
its citizens, honest and gentle,
won't fight among themselves
or keep a nut or a blade
of grass if it's not theirs.
Elephants, bears and tigers cross rivers
to attack other lands like his soldiers.
His subjects worship him as a god....

Waking up, he looks around
and finds a hollow under the linden
in which a nation of ants resides.
He drowns them in an ocean of urine.

A Mission

He was sent by our Emperor to the west
together with a hundred men,
to acquire the grand horses that
His Majesty had heard would sweat blood.
Also, it was reported that the Huns
had killed the king of a distant country
and made his skull into a wine bowl;
our Emperor ordered him to reach
that country and turn it into an ally
so we could use our enemies against each other.

On his way west the emissary was captured
and detained time and again.
He stayed four years among the Huns.
Later he escaped, continued his journey
and did find that remote country;
but its ruler had forgotten
the shame of his great-uncle's death—
never having heard of our empire
he refused to be our vassal.

Twenty-eight years later the emissary
returned, toothless, though
still followed by a tottering servant.
He brought back with him
a Bactrian wife, seven children,
and the "celestial horses" for
the emperor, who had died a decade before.
All his men had vanished in the desert,
but their lives were not totally wasted—
the loss led to our permanent policy:
Use barbarians to subdue barbarians.

Expedition

Again the grand eunuch was dispatched
into the Pacific with sixty-three ships
and twenty-eight thousand men
"to display our splendor and might
to all small kingdoms under heaven."
The Treasure Frigates were loaded
with porcelain, silk, silver and gold
so that he could purchase for the palace
rare creatures and objects, which would be
classified as tribute from new vassal states.
They sailed to North Australia, Java,
Sumatra, Siam, Ceylon, even entered
the Arabian Sea and Persian Gulf,
then turned south and reached East Africa
half a century before the Portuguese.

Wherever they dropped their stone anchors
the tall eunuch would assure the natives
that he demanded no trade,
no colonies, no land, no material gain.
All he wanted was a bought tribute
that acknowledged our superiority.
Dozens of kingdoms jumped at the bargain
and began to send their "tribute"
to Peking, where our imperial map
expanded every spring, except for
the kings of Palembang and Ceylon
who turned down our offer and claimed
they'd sooner have independence;
but both the stubborn men
were caught and brought back to China
to do obeisance to our Emperor in person.

Then a few Confucian ministers reproached
His Majesty for indulging in such
a costly pursuit of pleasure and vanity.
Before another voyage, the eunuch
was ordered to ground his fleet forever.
An undersecretary at court even burned
all his maps and logbooks, declaring
they were evil, "too outlandish to be true."

None of them imagined that
European caravels and galleons
would cleave the Indian Ocean
and pry open our shores.

Meeting the Barbarians

The First European

Having waited for twenty years,
preaching the Gospel along the coast,
poring over our classics at night,
finally he was summoned to Peking.
He brought along a map, a clock,
a breviary in a gold binding,
a cross adorned with gemstones,
a purse containing relics of saints,
two prisms, an hourglass, a clavichord,
and within him an essential Europe.

The sight of the Imperial Palace
disheartened him, as he realized
his paltry presents might not insure
an audience from Emperor Wan-Li.
He was right. His map was unacceptable.
How dare he put our Middle Kingdom
on the margin of the world
like a large island! He was made
to revise it, to restore our Empire
at the center of the universe.

Naturally the Emperor was not impressed
and ordered him sent back.
But before he mounted his camel
two eunuchs rushed in, asking him to
go to the court immediately
because the clock had stopped
and nobody knew how to make it run.
Chuckling, he believed this
to be God's intervention.

In the Forbidden City he took apart the clock
to show the eunuchs how to repair it

and how to wind and oil it.
He invented a word for every part.
Still none of the eunuchs could make
head or tail of the springs,
the gears, the perpetual pendulum.
They wondered why the clock,
unlike a peacock or a monkey,
didn't need feeding or grooming.

Then he was invited to teach them
how to play the clavichord.
Next he helped improve our calendar.
At a dinner he impressed the chancellors
by reciting poems backward after
reading them only twice.
He could do that even with a list
of forty names written in disorder.
All the young scholars present felt lucky
that this man was a foreign monk, or
he would surely have come out first
in the Royal Examination on classics.

The Emperor's messengers came every day
and asked him about the West's soil,
farming, birds, paintings, words,
hunting, architecture, cities,
astronomy, population, fishery.
So he stayed, provided with a stipend
and grain, though never allowed
to see the Emperor's pale face.
He built his church
whose steeple like a needle
punctured the sky of our capital.

On his deathbed he said to his fellow Europeans,
"I'm leaving you a door open
to great reward, but only after
dangers encountered and labors endured."

Etiquette

As only one sun rules heaven
there should be only one Emperor on earth.
How ignorant are those barbarians
who dare to claim to be our equals.
In King George's letter, he calls our Emperor
"My Dear Brother" and demands an embassy
in our capital and five trading ports.
More outrageous was his man named Macartney,
who refused to kowtow to the Son of Heaven
but claimed England, unlike Korea or Burma,
was the first monarch of the West,
so its envoy should be treated specially.
He refused to kneel on both knees before
our Emperor and declared he would do that
only in front of God or a woman.
He proposed to kiss our Emperor's
hand while kneeling on one knee only.
This was absolutely impossible—
no one should break the rite
or touch the body of the Holy Dragon.

Because he did not behave like those from
other states who knelt down three times
on both knees and knocked
their heads on the ground,
Macartney sailed back with nothing
but a letter from our Emperor
addressed to King George. It says:
"We are mindful of your tribute envoy's
ignorance and rude manners,
but we forgive him, you, and England,
considering that yours is a tiny state
in a waste corner of the world."

Actually the letter had been drafted
before Macartney's arrival.

Trade

The Sea Barbarians live by trade,
wanting in any high purpose.
For us, who have been self-sufficient
since heaven separated from earth,
trade is unnecessary.
They buy our tea, silk, porcelain, rhubarb
(with which they cleanse their bodies
and restore their spirits because
they eat too much milk and meat),
whereas we have no need for
their gadgets, calico, locomotives.

Many times they have complained
that the trade is unbalanced
and that we are unfair not to
allow them to do business inland.

This is our land.
We don't go to theirs.
Why do we have to let them in?
Is it our fault that their silver
has flowed out of their hands?
Why do they need to set up
consulates in four provinces?
Who ever heard the term "Inter-
national Law" or "trading port"?

We know they want to carve up our land
and suck out its marrow and grease.
That's why they came with warships
loaded with opium and troops.
They mean to drug and butcher
our Empire, which to them
is no more than a crippled dinosaur.

An Opium Smoker

After the eleventh pipe,
the idiot smile blooming on his face,
again he becomes boneless.
The naked stone slab beneath him
feels softer than eiderdown
while he's mounting the clouds.

He sees radiant palaces over rainbows,
a thousand ships carrying his soldiers,
under his orders columns of horses
charging forward, his generals
in the forms of lions and tigers.

For such glory, all he does is remain
tranquil in this filthy den,
oblivious of the other "skeletons"
around him and of those kept
in the morgue behind the house.

Wrapped in his heaven, for the moment
he has no ear for the sobbing
of his teenage daughter pawned
at a brothel for forty dollars,
but in a few hours he will again
twist like a possessed worm.

An Edict from the Empress Dowager

Last summer the Sea Barbarians
attempted to enter the Peiho River,
but in the twinkling of an eye
their ships were sunk
and thousands of bodies floating
in the water became food for fish.
I thought this lesson would teach them
to be more circumspect,
but they returned this year
more numerous and more insolent.

Taking advantage of the low tide
they disembarked at Pehtang
and then attacked Taku Forts.
Like true barbarians, they approached
the forts only from the rear.
Our soldiers, always meeting
their enemies face to face,
did not expect such perfidy.

Emboldened by the success that
should have shamed them,
they turned to seize Tientsin.
My anger is soaring to the clouds
and I want to have them exterminated.

Now, I command all my subjects,
Manchu, Chinese, Mongols,
to hunt them down like savage beasts.
Let your villages be abandoned
as these wretches come near.
Let your wells be poisoned
from which they draw water.
Let your crops be burned

before they can use them.
Let all provisions be destroyed
which they are eager to secure.

Thus they will perish
like shrimp in a frying pan.

Breach

The big-nosed barbarians claimed
they came for peace, but they brought
twenty thousand troops from the sea.
They meant to despoil our land,
so we fought them with every means.

To our surprise, they wanted to talk
of armistice and we agreed.
They dispatched a team of thirty-eight men,
who arrived calm and arrogant.
While they were resting in the square
our soldiers sprang at them like
eagles falling on chicks,
trussed them up, and carted them
to Peking under cover of night.

We displayed them in a market
where people spat on them, pulled
their noses, twisted their ears.
A young French devil asked for food,
but we fed him dung and dirt.
As for their Chinese coolies,
we buried them up to their necks,
let dogs eat their heads.

Within a week twenty devils died.
Our princes were so pleased
they gave each soldier a silver dollar
and the fearless captain a wife.

The barbarian generals accused us
of breaking our word of honor,
so their army smashed our cavalry
(their artillery was more accurate).

They marched into our capital
and entered the Summer Palace.

After all its treasures were plundered
Lord Elgin sent our Emperor a message
by torching his favorite park—
the smoke flying north
two hundred miles away
choked the Son of Heaven to death.

The Rebel Leaders

In a godless land every hero may become a god.
When Hong failed the examination again—
his dream of being an official shattered—
he was carried home and remained
in bed for days delirious, sweating, prattling.
He saw himself join God in heaven
where God's wife treated him as a son.
When he couldn't answer a seraph's question
a woman gave him a clue. He recognized her
as his sister-in-law, the wife of Jesus.
What a blissful place heaven was,
full of angels and buxom maidens.

As he returned to this world
he realized he belonged to God's family—
he was the youngest son sent down
to replace Christ, to cleanse earth
and redeem it for their Father.

He began to baptize people in the manner
prescribed in the pamphlet given him
by an old Protestant missionary.
After he gathered enough worshipers
he went to attack cities and towns,
his troops invincible and well-disciplined,
men and women kept in separate camps,
sex prohibited, even among married couples,
because the genuine union of men and women
could happen only after the final victory.

Within a year they took Nanking
which he turned into the Celestial Capital.
He set up a new calendar,
ordered his subjects to call him

the Sovereign, the ruler of the
Heavenly Kingdom of Great Peace.
They prepared to march north to Peking
to topple the Manchu Court.

But one of his generals, who used
to be a charcoal burner,
began to have trances and claimed
to be the Holy Ghost, speaking
in the very voice of the Father.
He ordered the Sovereign to kneel
in a square and be publicly flogged
as punishment for kicking a concubine
and spoiling his baby son.
The Sovereign obeyed.

A month later another general
began to get into trances
calling himself Jesus Christ.
The Sovereign had no choice but to
admit him into the divine household—
appointed him the West King,
allowed him to have a territory,
a staff, a harem, a band.

So they never crossed the Yellow River.
Even after the Kingdom collapsed
and the rebel leaders were destroyed
people would not depose them from heaven.
Their names are still
invoked in thousands of prayers.

Starting Off

The bell was tolling as fire
crackled in the pottery braziers.
Three hundred men gathered before the shrine
holding halberds, swords, shovels, forks.
A few knelt before the statue of
a local god, who had been a man
three generations ago and led people
to drive the Japanese pirates
back into the Pacific Ocean.
Above their shaved heads
white banners slanted in the breeze
which was full of chestnuts and beef.

An old man, the village head, fired a blank
at the naked chest of a young man,
then declared they were all divine soldiers
whose skin could block any foreign bullet.
Indeed the young man, unscratched,
only had a smudge on his nipple.
A Taoist priest went to the front
and announced that eleven million troops
would soon descend from heaven.
It was time to wipe out the foreign devils,
to reclaim China's sovereign land.

And so they set out, chanting:
"Give back our rivers and mountains.
Give back our silver and gold.
We dare to tread on knives and flames.
Even though the Emperor has surrendered
to foreigners, we won't stop,
not until we kill them off."

They headed to the nearby
church to decapitate
Christians like red poppies.

Help

At long last the Boxers were crushed,
but the foreign troops began looting.
The cities of Peking smelled of death,
bugles and screams filled the air.
Abandoned by the Manchu Court,
all we could do was wait for our doom.
Rich men had fled to the countryside
with their wives and concubines,
their homes littered with bodies of
their servants and poor relatives
hanged or drowned in wells.
Like most people, I stayed in town
and prayed the Lord of Heaven would rain mercy.

A friend of mine said the Americans were
better than the other barbarians.
(The French, the British, the Russians
knew nothing but metal and stones;
they smashed and burned the treasures
that they couldn't turn into cash.)
So when an American marine came
I gave him ten tins of oolong tea
and begged him to write a notice
that might help protect my grocery.

His olive eyes winked at me
as his hairy fingers pulled at his nose.
On a piece of rice paper he wrote:
"USA Boys—plenty of tobacco
and whiskey in this shop."

I posted the notice on the front door,
but it didn't stop any troops.
A group of Frenchmen burst in

and ordered me to give them whiskey,
which I didn't know where to get.
They knocked me to the ground,
kicked my face, seized our hens
and took my daughter away.

An Execution

The criminals to be executed
had killed two German missionaries.
The German soldiers in helmets
didn't know how to use our swords
or maybe they were afraid of
being stained by pagan blood.
They stood in rows, rifles in hand,
their boots shiny in the sun,
their flag flapping noisily.

Three Chinese in black aprons
worked as a team, one pulling
the kneeling man's pigtail, another
holding his bound hands from behind,
the third raising a crescent sword
still steaming with blood.
The criminal prayed to his ancestors,
then cried, "In thirty years
I'll be back as a warrior to kill
the foreign devils and all of you,
their shameless flunkeys!"
Beside him lay his cousin, whose head
was twenty yards away before
a British officer's feet.

In silence hundreds of Chinese watched—
a boy astride his father's neck,
a toothless man sucking a pipe,
ladies waving fans under the parasols
raised by their servants.
None of them looked at the falling
sword, all their eyes
focused on a foreigner's camera.

The Victory

When Prince Chun was sent to Germany
to apologize for the assassination
of Baron von Ketteler, the Germans
wanted him to kowtow at the Kaiser's feet
in addition to offering them
Shandong province, an indemnity of
one hundred million taels of gold
and railroad concessions.

Adamantly our prince refused to
prostrate himself before Wilhelm,
saying to his entourage,
"Our Empire cannot demean her honor."
To his surprise, the Germans,
so pleased with what they did get,
forgot his knees.

On his return, a victory banquet
was held at court for
the national face he had saved.
Later his three-year-old son
was chosen to be our Emperor, the last.

A Ghost's Argument

In our history books, I am a criminal
condemned for not fortifying Canton
when the British ships gathered on the sea.
But I never tried to pacify the enemy either,
refusing their demands again and again.
In their eyes I was a joke
and a monster; European newspapers
called me the Barbarian Governor.

When they came to attack the city
I didn't fight, so they prevailed easily.
They waited on the highland for me to
capitulate, but I never showed up.
Out of patience, they scoured streets,
districts, sampans, monasteries,
finally dragged me out from a local
law office and took me to their flagship.

I thought they'd execute me on the spot,
but they said it would not be so easy for me.
They shipped me to Calcutta,
where I died of dropsy
and homesickness in a cell.
Thank heaven, they didn't take me
farther west to Europe.

Children of the future, remember
me as a wronged ghost.
It's true I was a passive man.
But what else could I have done to save
the city from being sacked?
Was there any way to stop their warships?
Better just to bluff them, so that
our court wouldn't blame me for

not resisting the enemy force
and annihilate my clan when I was gone.

It's true I was a coward, to whom
honor and bravery were mere phantoms.
But children of the future, remember
that I died alone—unlike
heroes and generals, I didn't take
other souls underground with me.

Departure

Having put their baggage away in the cabin
they gathered at the prow, where
wine and roast duck were waiting.

Thirty-two students were about to cross
the oceans for the first time
in our Empire. Among them
were would-be experts in
weaponry, metallurgy, politics,
law, architecture, philosophy.

The air smelled of coal,
purple clouds hanging on the coast,
seagulls flitting,
a few petrels twittering in the smoke.

Together they emptied their cups
and swore they'd study hard to master
all the knowledge in the West
so that their Motherland would not need
to send youths abroad again.

Their tears were shed only for the wind.
None of them knew
that this was just a beginning—
that their children would travel
the same seas.

Note

The following books provided information used in some of these poems:

Bloodworth, Dennis & Ching Ping. *The Chinese Machiavelli.* New York: Dell, 1976.

Cameron, Nigel. *Barbarians and Mandarins.* New York: Walker/Weatherhill, 1970.

Han Fei Tzu. *Basic Writing.* Trans. by Burton Watson. New York: Columbia University Press, 1964.

Horn, Joshua. *Away with All Pets.* New York: Monthly Review Press, 1969.

Levy, Howard. *Chinese Footbinding.* New York: W. Rawls, 1966.

Sima, Qian. *Records of the Grand Historian.* Trans. by Burton Watson. New York: Columbia University Press, 1993.

Sinclair, Kevin. *The Yellow River: A 5000-Year Journey Through China.* Los Angeles, CA: The Knapp Press, 1987.

Varé, Daniele. *The Last Empress.* New York: Doubleday, 1938.